Moira Miller
MERRY-MA-TANZIE

The Playbook Treasury

Illustrated by
Doreen Caldwell

Here we go round the jingo-ring,
The jingo-ring, the jingo-ring,
Here we go round the jingo-ring,
About the Merry-ma-tanzie.

Books for Children
in association with
Methuen Children's Books

The publishers wish to acknowledge the kind
permission of the following to include their
copyright material:

Atheneum Publishers for *After a Bath* by Aileen
Fisher and *Waking* by Lilian Moore

Curtis Brown Ltd, London & New York, for
Winter Morning by Ogden Nash, copyright ©
1961, 1962 Ogden Nash

E P Dutton, a division of NAL Penguin Inc,
McClelland and Stewart, Toronto and Methuen
Children's Books, London for *Furry Bear* and
Wind on the Hill from *Now We Are Six* by A A
Milne. Copyright 1927 by E P Dutton,
renewed 1955 by A A Milne; and for *Happiness*
from *When We Were Very Young* by A A Milne.
Copyright 1924 by E P Dutton, renewed 1952
by A A Milne

Harper and Row for *Close Your Eyes* and *Leaf Buds*
by Aileen Fisher

Hodder & Stoughton (Australia) Pty Ltd for *The
Christmas Pudding* by Jean Chapman, 1977

Houghton Mifflin Company for *Seashell* from *The
Complete Works of Amy Lowell*, copyright ©
1955 by Houghton Mifflin Company, copyright
© 1983 renewed by Houghton Mifflin
Company, Brinton P Robers, Esq and G
D'Andelot Belin, Esq

The James Reeves Estate for *Beech Leaves*, ©
James Reeves Estate

The Society of Authors, as the literary
representative of the Estate of Rose Fyleman,
and Doubleday, New York for *Witch, Witch* by
Rose Fyleman

Every effort has been made to trace owners of
copyright material, but in some cases this has not
proved possible. The publishers would be glad to
hear from any further copyright owners of material
reproduced in *Merry-ma-tanzie*.

First published in Great Britain in 1987
by Methuen Children's Books Ltd
11 New Fetter Lane, London EC4P 4EE
Text copyright © 1987 Moira Miller
Illustrations copyright © 1987 Doreen Caldwell

Printed in Hong Kong by South China Printing Co

ISBN 0 416 46860 8

CONTENTS

I pegged my washing on the line,
On a bright and windy day,
I pushed the pegs down hard and
tight,
But the washing flew away.

Over the rooftop, over the wall,
And over the trees so green.
And though we searched both
high and low,
My washing's never been seen.

MOIRA MILLER

WAKING

My secret way of waking
is like a place
to hide.
I'm very still,
my eyes are shut.
They all think I am sleeping
but
I'm wide awake inside.

They all think I am sleeping
but I'm wiggling my toes.
I feel sun fingers
on my cheeks.
I hear voices whisper-speak.
I squeeze my eyes
to keep them shut
so they will think I'm
sleeping
BUT
I'm really wide awake inside
– and no one knows!

LILIAN MOORE

4

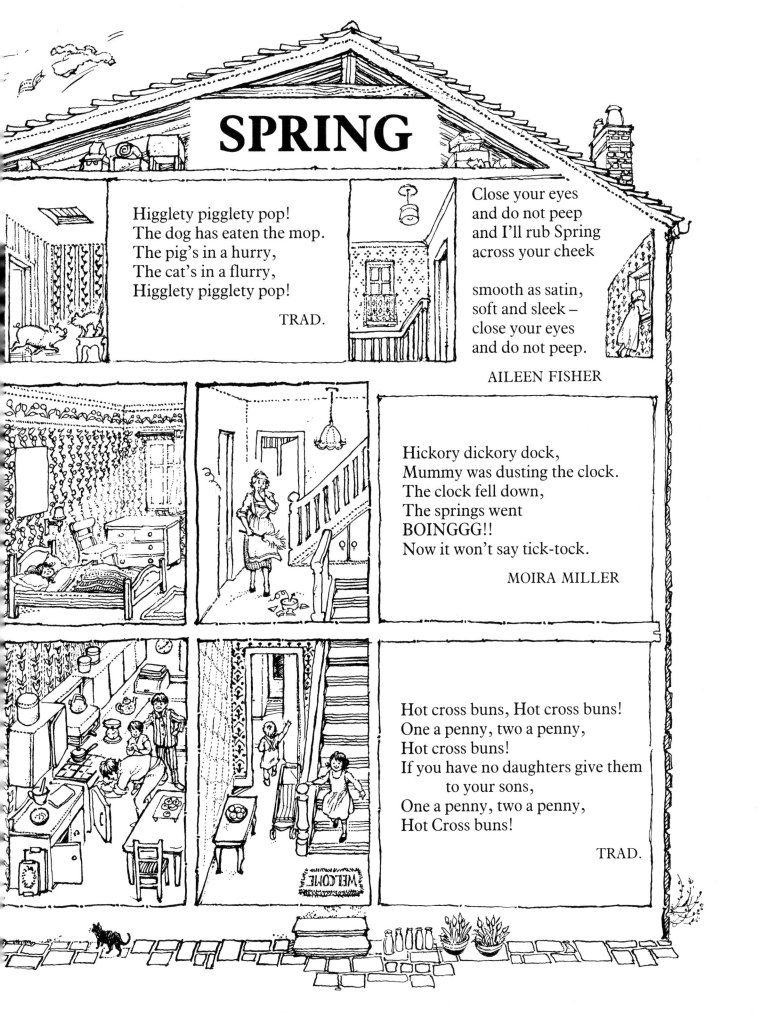

SPRING

Higglety pigglety pop!
The dog has eaten the mop.
The pig's in a hurry,
The cat's in a flurry,
Higglety pigglety pop!

TRAD.

Close your eyes
and do not peep
and I'll rub Spring
across your cheek

smooth as satin,
soft and sleek –
close your eyes
and do not peep.

AILEEN FISHER

Hickory dickory dock,
Mummy was dusting the clock.
The clock fell down,
The springs went
BOINGGG!!
Now it won't say tick-tock.

MOIRA MILLER

Hot cross buns, Hot cross buns!
One a penny, two a penny,
Hot cross buns!
If you have no daughters give them
to your sons,
One a penny, two a penny,
Hot Cross buns!

TRAD.

Let's go down to the park today.
How many children have come to play?
How many ducks on the pond can you see?
Count them slowly, one, two, three.

Look at the park when it starts to rain.
Come on, Mum, hurry home again!
What do you think – is it too wet to stay?
You can always come back another day.

Plants

Do plants eat and drink?
Of course they do.
But not like me –
And not like you!

No, not like that!
Plants use their roots,
And drink through their boots!

There's something else
a plant needs too.
Plenty of sunshine – all day through!

Let's find out what happens
to plants if they don't have
water or sunshine. Let's do an
EXPERIMENT!

Seeds Needs

Ask Mum to save three
polystyrene trays. Lay a piece of
kitchen paper in each tray and sprinkle
them all with some cress seeds.
Pour a little water into two of the
trays to wet the paper and put all
three into a dark cupboard.

Look at them again two days later.
What has happened?
Do you know why?

If you put the two that are
growing in a sunny place and
water them again they will get even
bigger and begin to turn green.
Seeds like sunshine.

Pop the third one back in the
cupboard and water it this time.
It will soon catch up with the
others.

9

Lunch Munch

Now you have grown all that cress what can you do with it? Well – you could make some sandwiches.

You will need:
2 slices of bread, butter, cress, salt, and one knife – make sure it's not too sharp.

Ask Mum to help you to spread butter on the bread. Pull the green tops and stems off the cress plants – don't eat the seeds – and lay them on one slice of bread. Sprinkle a little salt on the cress and top it with the other slice.

Cut up your sandwich and eat it for lunch. Yum! Perhaps Mum or Dad would like one too.

Don't forget to help with the washing up when you have finished making your sandwiches.

Bubble Pictures

Put a little water in a plastic cup. Squeeze in
some washing up liquid and two or three
drops of food colouring. It can be any colour
you like. Put a plastic straw in the cup and

BLOW!!!

If you press a piece of white paper on top of
the cup very quickly before the bubbles pop
you can print a picture of them.

Shhhhh – listen! Can you hear all your bubbles popping?

Don't forget to wash the cup out when you have finished!

The Runaway Pancake

Once upon a time – yesterday, or the day before – Mum was in the kitchen making tea.

"Goodness me," she said. "What can I make to feed those seven hungry little boys of mine."

"Sausages," said one.

"Fish fingers," said the second.

"Beans on toast," said the third.

"Pie," said the fourth.

"Jelly," said the fifth.

"Beefburgers," said the sixth, and

"Ba ba ba," said the baby – but he LOOKED hungry.

"I can't make any of those things," said Mum. "All I have are some big round brown eggs, a jug of milk and some flour. I shall make a pancake."

So Mum took her big round blue bowl and put in some flour. Whumph!

She broke in the big round brown eggs.

One.

Two.

Three.

And she poured in the milk. Clubba-lubba-lubba. And then she mixed and mixed and mixed, until the bowl was full of runny golden pancake mix.

She popped some fat in the pan and put it on the cooker. Sizzle-dizzle, sizzle-dizzle went the hot fat.

"Now I can make my pancake," said Mum. And she poured in the runny golden pancake mix.

Mmmmm, what a lovely smell it made. Mum tipped the pan and the runny mix spread all over the bottom in a big round pancake shape.

"It's beginning to set," said Mum, and quick as a flip she turned the pancake over.

"Oooo," thought the pancake. "That was hot!"

"I'd like a BIG piece," said the first little boy.

"And me too," said the second.

"Me too," said the third.

"And I," said the fourth.

"Don't forget ME," said the fifth.

"I want some too," said the sixth.

"Ba ba ba," said the baby, but he LOOKED hungry.

"I'll cut it up in just a tick," said Mum and she put the plates on the table. One, two, three, four, five, six, and a little bowl for the baby.

"Oh no you won't!" said the pancake, and while she was looking for the forks he jumped WHIZZ BANG right out of the pan and rolled across the floor like a big round golden penny.

"Come back here," said Mum, chasing after the pancake.

"Come back!" shouted all the hungry little boys, jumping up and down.

"Ba ba ba," shouted the baby, but he SOUNDED hungry.

The big round golden pancake ran right out of the door and down the path. It rolled down and round the corner past the lollipop lady at the crossing.

"I do feel hungry," said the lollipop lady. "Come back I want to eat you!" She dropped her big round lollipop and ran after Mum and the seven little boys.

"Oh no you don't!" said the big round pancake. And he rolled down the road faster and faster. He passed a man who was digging a hole.

"Goodness," said the man, "I've only got sandwiches to eat and that pancake looks very tasty." He dropped his spade and ran after Mum and her seven little boys and the lollipop lady.

"Come back," he shouted. "I want to eat you."

"Oh no you don't," said the big round pancake and it rolled down the road faster and faster. He rolled zippety quick round the corner and through a garden gate.

There was a big brown dog lying on the path.

"Hello," said the big brown dog, sniffing. "I smell food. What a beautiful big round pancake. I am going to gobble you all up."

"Oh no you don't," said the pancake.

"Oh yes I will," said the big brown dog. And quick as a wink – he did. He licked up every crumb of that big round golden pancake. Mum and the seven little boys and the lollipop lady and the man who was digging the hole stood and watched.

"Never mind," said Mum. "Let's all go home and make another pancake." So that is what they did.

But this time, to make sure it wouldn't roll away, Mum cooked a SQUARE pancake.

Easter Nests

You will need: one shredded wheat biscuit, four squares of chocolate, 2 oz of marzipan, paper cake cases, teaspoon, small bowl.

Break up the squares of chocolate and try not to eat any! Put them in a bowl and ask Mum to stand the bowl in a pan of hot water. Watch carefully! The chocolate will very slowly melt until you can stir it with a spoon. Crumble up the shredded wheat and stir it into the chocolate. Spoon the chocolate covered shredded wheat into the cake cases and make a dent in the middle. You have made a little chocolate nest!

Leave the chocolate to set hard. Roll some marzipan eggs and pop them into the nests. Does everyone have one for tea?

Happy Easter!

Chook, chook, chook, chook, chook,
Good morning, Mrs Hen.
How many chickens have you got?
Madam, I've got ten.
Four of them are yellow,
And four of them are brown,
And two of them are speckled red,
The nicest in the town.

TRAD.

I know a little pussy,
Her coat is silver grey;
She lives down in the meadow,
Not very far away.
Although she is a pussy,
She'll never be a cat,
For she's a pussy willow –
Now what do you think of that?

TRAD.

Have you ever seen pussy willow buds growing! Next time you go out
look for some that are closed up tight. Pick a twig – just one – and put it
water when you get home. Watch what happens!

Patch Box

Help Mum to find a big shallow box with a lid. Perhaps the supermarket would have one.

Divide it up inside with strips of card or other small boxes. Can you make them fit?

Fill up your Patch Box with sweet papers, scraps of wool, coloured cloth, milk top lids (but remember to wash them first) or anything else you would like to collect.

You can use your Patch Box to play

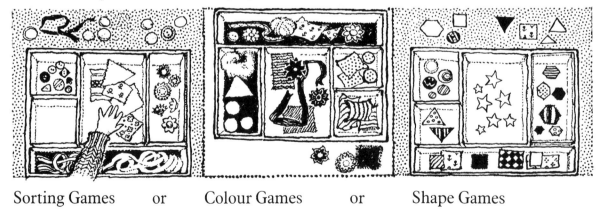

Sorting Games   or   Colour Games   or   Shape Games

Why not make up some games of your own, or use your Patch Box to make a sticky picture.

Sticky Pictures

Sticky pictures are best if you make them on stiff paper.

Like wallpaper

Or wrapping paper

. . . but not when it's still on the wall!

. . . but not if there's still a parcel inside it!

Use a good thick paste. You can spread it on with a spreader made from a strip of thick cardboard. Choose your patches and stick them down carefully to make a bright picture. But don't forget to cover the table with old newspapers first, and do wear an apron.

Make yourself a Great Big Sticky Picture. Do you know anyone else who would like one too?

Painting Pictures

You will need: one tin of poster paint powder, one large fat brush, a big sheet of stiff paper, and an empty washing-up liquid bottle.

Pull the cap off the washing-up liquid bottle and wash it out. Ask Mum to cut off the top 8 cm.

Put three teaspoonfuls of powder paint into the bottom of the bottle and mix it with a little cold water. Don't make it too runny!

Push the top in upside down and pop your brush through the hole. Now you're ready to paint and even if you knock the pot over the paint won't spill.

Don't forget to cover the table with old newspapers and be sure to wear an overall!

Sunshine Faces

It's good to see the sun in Springtime. Sometimes it's bright and warm.
Sometimes it can only just peep out through the rain clouds.

Sunshine Smile Face

Sunshine Sad Face

It's very easy to make your own Sunshine Face. You will need: a white
paper plate, yellow poster paint, crayons, cotton wool and paste.

Paint the plate yellow on both sides and leave it to dry.

On one side use your crayons to
draw a Sunshine Smile Face.

On the other side draw a
Sunshine Sad Face and stick on
some cotton wool rain clouds.

Can you think of any other Sunshine Faces to make?

Puppet People

What is a puppet? A puppet is not like a teddy bear.

You play with a Teddy Bear . . .

but a puppet plays with you!

There are all sorts of puppets.

Some are very **big.**

Some are very small.

Some have strings.

Some are only shadows.

They are all fun to play with. Let's make some. All you will need is a hand and some felt pens.

Hello Finger Family!

More Potty Puppets

Use felt pens or crayons to draw
a face on a small paper bag.
Twist the corners up
to make ears.

Make your own Spooky Spider
with sticky circles on the back of
an old woolly glove. Eeek!

Dress up thin Mrs Wooden Spoon with a duster and some sellotape.

Here is a rhyme to act with your finger puppets. Start with your two fat
thumbs and finish with your two little fingers.

Two fat gentlemen met in a lane,
Bowed most politely, bowed once again.
How do you do?
How do you do?
And how do you do again?

Two thin ladies met in a lane . . .

Two tall policemen met in a lane . . .

Two little schoolboys met in a lane . . .

Two little babies met in a lane,
Bowed most politely, bowed once again.
How do you do?
How do you do?
And how do you do again?

A Great Big Super

Perhaps all your friends from Playgroup or Nursery School could help you to make this picture. Mix up a pot of green paint to make stems for the grass and daffodils. Make the flowers with yellow paper petals and yellow

All winter in the tree buds
The little leaves lie packed
With tiny coats of April green,
All folded and exact.

And when the time is ready
(I wonder how they know?)
They quietly unfold themselves
And break the buds and grow.

AILEEN FISHER

A little green frog in a pond am I,
Hoppity hoppity hop.
I sit on a little leaf, high
   and dry,
And watch all the fishes as they
   swim by –
Splash! How I make the water fly!
Hoppity hoppity hop.

TRAD.

Can you make up actions
to go with this poem?

Spring Picture

or white egg box sections cut up. They will stick on easily with thick paste. That great big brown paper Easter Bunny has a lovely soft cotton wool tail. Could you make a yellow cotton wool chicken too?

A little brown rabbit popped out of the ground,
Wriggled his whiskers and looked around.
Another wee rabbit who lived in the grass
Popped his head out and watched him pass.

Then both the wee rabbits went hoppity hop,
Hoppity, hoppity, hoppity hop,
Till they came to a wall and had to stop.
Then both the wee rabbits turned themselves
    round,
And scuttled off home to their holes in the ground.

TRAD.

Could your fingers be rabbit puppets for this poem?

Hickety pickety my black hen,
She lays eggs for gentlemen.
Gentlemen come every day,
To see what my black hen doth lay.
Sometimes nine and sometimes ten,
Hickety pickety my black hen.

TRAD.   23

Sam's Super Spuds

Dad was digging in the back garden.

Whoof! went the fork into the dark brown earth.

Heave! went Dad as he lifted it up.

Thudump! went the forkful of thick dark earth as he turned it over.

"What are you doing?" asked Sam. Dad stopped and leaned on his fork.

"Cutting the grass," he said.

"No you're not!" laughed Sam. "You're digging!"

"Well then," said Dad. "If you know what I'm doing, why ask?" He went on digging. Whoof, heave, thudump. Whoof, heave, thudump.

"But why are you?" asked Sam.

"Digging?" said Dad. "Because I'm going to plant some spuds here, and I have to make the bed for them."

"Make the bed?" said Sam laughing. "For potatoes?"

"Of course," said Dad. "You wouldn't like it if your bed was all lumpy would you? Spuds are just the same. They like a nice soft bed too. Come and help me tuck them in."

The potatoes were in a big brown paper bag. Dad and Sam counted them out and Dad marked four rows with his fork.

"Right," he said. "Ten potatoes in each row." Very carefully Sam counted them.

"One, two, three, four, five, six, seven, eight, nine, ten."

Dad started to cover the potatoes with earth.

"Why do you do that?" said Sam.

"Tuck them in all comfy cosy," said Dad.

"Then they can go to sleep?" said Sam.

"That's right," said Dad. "And when we dig them up again they'll be ready to eat."

"Good night, spuds," whispered Sam, and he helped Dad to cover all the little potatoes with thick dark earth.

Next morning Sam went out to the garden to see what the potatoes were doing.

"Nothing's happened," he said.

"Give it time," said Mum. "Potatoes don't like to do things in a hurry."

Every morning Sam went out to the garden. Every morning it was the same.

"Nothing there," said Sam. "Do you think the potatoes know how to grow?"

"'Course they do," said Mum. "But they're just like you, they do it slowly when nobody's watching!"

After a time Sam forgot to look at the potatoes every morning. Then one day Dad came in from the garden.

"Have you seen those spuds?" he said. "They're getting really big now."

Sam ran out to look. In all four rows there were ten little plants with bright green leaves.

"Where are the potatoes?" he said.

"Still in bed," said Dad. "That's just their tops peeping out. They're not big enough to get up yet." He went along the rows of potatoes with his hoe, taking out some little weeds that had grown between them.

"Must keep them neat," he said. "You can't sleep in an untidy bed."

"I do!" said Sam.

"That's true," said Dad. "But you're not a potato!"

The potato plants grew bigger and bigger. Some days it was sunny and Sam pretended they were trees and hid his toy soldiers in among them. Other days it rained, and the leaves were all wet and droopy.

"Never mind," said Dad. "Rain's good for them. It'll help the little spuds grow big and fat."

The small green plants became big green plants, and the tiny flowers opened out bright and white like stars. Sam could hardly see the dark brown earth any more. It looked as if the bed was covered with a thick bright green quilt.

"Is it time for the potatoes to get up yet?" he asked.

"Not yet," said Mum. "It's still too early."

Sam and Mum and Dad went on holiday for two weeks. The morning after they came back Sam ran out to look at the potatoes.

"Something's happened to them!" he shouted running into the house. "They've gone all funny."

"Let's have a look," said Dad. The big bright green potato plants were yellow and floppy. The bed looked crumpled and untidy.

"Aha," said Dad, fetching his garden fork and a plastic bowl from the garage. "Time to get up."

Whoof! went the fork into the dark brown earth.

Heave! Dad lifted it up.

Thudump, thudump, THUDUMP! He turned over the fork and instead of just dark brown earth and one small potato there were lots and lots of round muddy lumps. Dad picked one up, brushed off the earth and there was a beautiful big round golden potato.

"How about that?" said Dad.

"There's another!" said Sam and he found a really huge one. Dad and Sam dug out all the potatoes that he'd grown from that one little plant and put them in the bowl. They washed them in the sink and spread them all out on the kitchen table.

Sam put them in a row with the very biggest potato at one end, and the very smallest one (that was just the size of a marble) at the other end. There were lots of them, too many for him to count.

"Super spuds!" said Mum. "There's plenty for dinner."

"And there are lots more that haven't got up yet!" said Sam.

"When they do," said Dad, "we'll save some to pop back into bed for next year."

Spring Cleaning

How many things can you help to spring clean?

Can you wash dishes?

Can you sweep?

Are you good at dusting?

Do you keep your toys tidy?

I wonder if you can polish
your shoes?

It's not easy to make a bed!

Can you spring clean yourself too?

Round About Me

Are you as big as Mum and Dad? Are you bigger than the baby? Is the dog bigger than you? Let's find out.

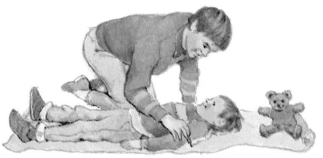

Lie down on a strip of old wallpaper that is longer than you are. Now ask someone to draw round you with a crayon or felt pen. Try not to wriggle if it tickles!

Now you've got a picture that's just the same size as you are. Does it look like you?

Draw a face with crayons or paints and dress your friend up with stuck on wool or paper.

Can you see who's the biggest person in the family? Are you the smallest in your family?

Here we go round the paddling pool,
The paddling pool, the paddling pool.
Here we go round the paddling pool,
On a sunny summer's day.

This is the way we kick and splash,
Kick and splash, kick and splash.
This is the way we kick and splash,
On a sunny summer's day.

This is the way we swim around,
Swim around, swim around.
This is the way we swim around,
On a sunny summer's day.

This is the way we sail our boats,
Sail our boats, sail our boats.
This is the way we sail our boats,
On a sunny summer's day.

This is the way we dry our toes,
Dry our toes, dry our toes.
This is the way we dry our toes,
On a sunny summer's day.

Here we go round the paddling pool,
The paddling pool, the paddling pool.
Here we go round the paddling pool,
On a sunny summer's day.

MOIRA MILLER

Rain on the green grass,
And rain on the tree,
Rain on the house-top,
But not on me!

TRAD.

Mary, Mary, quite contrary,
How does your garden grow?
With silver bells and cockle shells,
And pretty maids all in a row.

28

SUMMER

Sally go round the sun,
Sally go round the moon,
Sally go round the chimney pots,
On a Saturday afternoon.

Lavender's Blue, diddle
diddle,
Lavender's Green.
When I am king, diddle,
diddle,
You shall be queen.

TRAD.

Ipsey Wipsey spider,
Climbing up the spout,
Down came the rain,
And washed the spider
out.

Out came the sunshine,
And dried up all the rain,
Ipsey Wipsey spider,
Climbing up again.

Let's go down to the park today.
How many children have come to play?
How many ducks on the pond can you see?
Count them slowly, one, two, three.

Look at the park when it starts to rain.
Come on, Mum, hurry home again!
What do you think, is it too wet to stay?
You can always come back another day.

Vegetable Soup

There are lots of vegetables on this stall. Can you find the carrots? Where are the onions? Which one is the lettuce? Do you know what all the others are called?

If you help Mum to buy some vegetables you can make your own Summertime Vegetable Soup.

You will need:
1 onion,
2 carrots,
1 stick of celery,
2 chicken stock cubes,
2 pints of hot water.

Cut the tops off the carrots and put them to one side, then help Mum to scrub and cut up the carrots and celery into thin slices. Be very careful with that knife please! Peel the papery skin off the onion and cut it up too. Did it make you cry? Never mind. Ask Mum to heat a little cooking oil in the bottom of a big pan and cook the vegetables for five minutes. Crumble the stock cubes in hot water, stir them in and pour the water very carefully on to the vegetables. Now ask her to heat your soup until it is boiling, turn the heat down until it is just bubbling gently, put a lid on and leave it for an hour.

Mmm! Does it taste good? Perhaps it needs a little salt. If you like you could have *two* platefuls.

Carrot Top Islands

Did you remember to keep your carrot tops? You can make them into little treasure islands very easily. Stand them in a saucer of water on a sunny window sill for two or three days and watch the trees grow. Remember to add more water as it dries out.

You could try growing parsnip and turnip tops too.

I wonder who will visit your treasure islands. Will they be sailors, fishermen or even pirates?

Fish and Ships

Why not build your own ship? How many different cardboard boxes can you bring home from the supermarket?

What will you build? Could it be . . .

a supertanker?

A fishing boat?

A lifeboat?

Or even a pirate ship?

If you cut out cardboard fish and put metal paper clips on their noses you can catch them with string and a magnet. Ooooooh, help – I think that one's a shark!!

Sea Songs

Sea Shell

Sea Shell, Sea Shell,
Sing me a song, O please.
A song of ships, and sailor men,
And parrots, and tropical trees,
Of islands lost in the Spanish Main,
Which no man ever may find again,
Of fishes and corals under the waves,
And sea horses stabled in great green caves.

AMY LOWELL

A sailor went to sea, sea, sea,
To see what he could see, see, see,
But all that he could see, see, see,
Was the bottom of the deep blue sea, sea, sea.

TRAD.

Little Betty Blue,
Lost her holiday shoe.
What can little Betty do?
Give her another
To match the other,
And then she may walk out in two.

TRAD.

At the Seaside

When I was down beside the sea,
A wooden spade they gave to me
To dig the sandy shore.
My holes were empty like a cup,
In every hole the sea came up,
Till it could come no more.

ROBERT LOUIS STEVENSON

35

The Particular Seagull

It was lovely at the seaside. There were children playing on the beach and mums and dads lying in deck chairs in the sunshine, enjoying a quiet snooze.

Above their heads a sparkling white seagull was flying high in the sky.

"Oooooh look!" shouted the children. "Isn't he the most beautiful seagull you've ever seen?" They broke up their sandwiches and biscuits and threw pieces to him. The big white seagull, showing off like anything, swooped and dived, scooped up the bread and with a flap of his wings was off again to the harbour.

There, sitting at the end of the old stone pier, staring out to sea, sat a very scruffy seagull. His yellow feet were muddy and his feathers had a sort of greyish-brown unwashed look about them. The white seagull circled him twice, looking for a clean place to land, then came down with a great fluttering of wings.

"Very fine day," he said.

"Arrrrrr," said the scruffy seagull.

"Fishing boats are filthy, messy things," said the sparkling white seagull, wiping his feet on a piece of seaweed. He looked sideways down his beak at the scruffy seagull's dirty feet and feathers.

"Arrrrrr," said the scruffy seagull, shifting from one leg to the other.

"Food's much better too," said the white seagull. "Why, only last week someone threw me a ham and pickle sandwich. None of your common old herring for me. I'm going back for some cake now. Care to join me?"

"Arrrrrr," said the scruffy seagull, shaking his head.

All summer the holiday children threw bread and biscuits and pieces of cake to the white gull.

The children shouted with delight as he caught the scraps and threw him even more food.

The scruffy seagull hung round the boats to pick up whatever the fishermen threw away.

"Yuck, that's a fish head you're eating!" the white seagull said, turning up his beak in disgust.

"Aaaaaar," said the scruffy seagull, his beak full of fish.

"You wouldn't find me picking up things like that," said the white gull. "I'm particular about what I eat. I am a very particular seagull."

The summer days became colder, the blue sea was grey and choppy. One by one the holiday boats began to leave. The mums, dads and children left too.

"Goodbye, see you next year!" shouted the children to the white seagull.

He found it more and more difficult to get food, and had to search everywhere among the boats and along the beach. He became thinner and thinner and his fine feathers stuck out untidy and ruffled. He had to hunt further and further for food.

All this time the fishing boats came and went from the old stone pier and the

scruffy seagull sat waiting and watching.

At last, after two days without a scrap of food the white seagull flopped down and landed at the end of the stone pier. There was a loud gurgle as his empty tummy rumbled.

"Pardon!" he said.

"Arrrrrr," said the scruffy seagull. He turned his head into the wind and settled down on his great dirty feet, fluffing out his grey feathers around his well-fed stomach.

"I see the fishing boats are out," said the sparkling white seagull. "Er . . . think they'll be back soon?"

"Arrrr," said the scruffy gull. He hunched his head down into his shoulders and went to sleep. The white gull huddled beside him, trying to shelter from the cold sea wind.

And then at last, round the point, heading for the harbour came the first of the fishing boats, with a hold full of herrings that you could smell on the wind. The scruffy gull unfolded his wings and leapt into the wind to meet them.

"Mind if I join you?" shouted the white seagull, struggling to keep up. The scruffy gull's answer was lost, blown away on the wind. He was already half-way to the fishing boats.

Next summer the holiday makers came back: the mums, the dads and the children with their buckets and spades. They searched everywhere for the sparkling white seagull.

"Do you remember him?" they asked. "He used to catch the scraps we threw to him. He was a particularly beautiful bird. I wonder where he went."

Nobody noticed that there were now two scruffy seagulls sitting on the end of the dirty old pier waiting for the fishing boats to come back with their holds full of herring. They were two very fat and well-fed birds, and one of them was a *particularly* scruffy seagull.

Teddy Bears' Picnic

If you go down in the woods today,
You'd better go in disguise.
If you go down in the woods today,
You're sure of a big surprise.
For every bear that ever there was,
Is gathered there for certain because
Today's the day the Teddy Bears have
   their picnic!

What will you take to eat at the Teddy Bears' Picnic?

Honey Sandwiches

Spread the bread very
carefully with butter
and honey. Mmmm!
Sticky bears.

Bears' Paws

Make brown bread
sandwiches
with Marmite and cut
them into paws with
a biscuit cutter.

Teddy's Treat

Stir two teaspoonfuls
of chocolate instant
pudding
into a glass of milk.
Let it sit for a
little while and then
drink it up. Yum!!

And don't forget to take lots of apples – bears love apples.

Bearhunt

Let's go on a bearhunt. Kneel down and pat your hands on your knees to make the sounds. Ready, steady . . .

Off we go, down the road – *pad, pad, pad,*
Up the hill, slower and slower – *padump padump,*
And down the other side – *pitter, patter, pitter.*

On we go along the road, *pad, pad, pad.*
Oh dear! A river – we can't swim across,
We can't build a boat,
Let's take a run and jump across.
Ready? *Pitter, patter, pitter, patter,*
Wheeeeeeee! You made it without falling in!
Well done.

On we go along the road, *pad, pad, pad.*
Through the long grass – rub your hands together –
Swish, swish, swish, swish.
Through the squishy squashy bog – *sloosh, sloosh, sloosh,*
Up the hill – *padump, padump, padump.*

And here's the cave. It's very dark – shut your eyes.
Can you feel the cold, slimy, slippery wall?
And what's this?
It's BIG and SOFT and FURRY!!
Quick back down the hill, run fast,
Through the squishy bog, and the long grass.
Across the river – *Wheeeeeeee!*
And shut the door – SLAM-BANG!

Would you like to go on another Bearhunt? Let's leave it till tomorrow.

Paper Houses

What sort of house do you live in? Is it like . . .

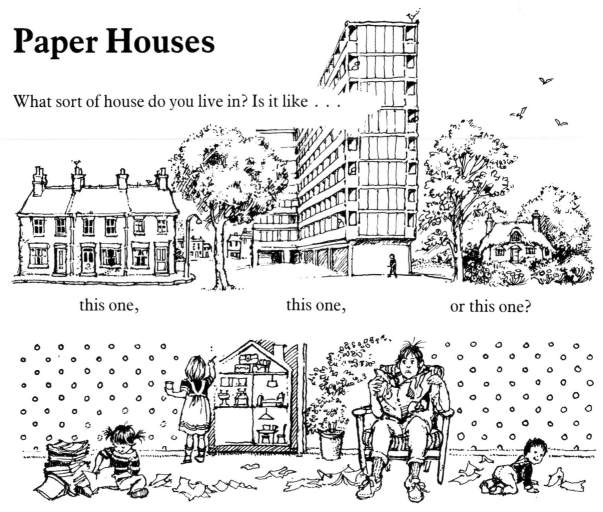

this one,   this one,   or this one?

You can make your very own paper house. Ask Mum to help you cut out a big house shape in stiff paper. Draw in the rooms with a thick black crayon.
Now your house is ready for furniture. Cut some out of old magazines and use your paste to stick them into the rooms.

What does your house look like?

Does it really have
three kitchens?   Or SIX bathrooms!!   WOW! That's some
block of flats!

Don't forget to ask if it's all right to cut out the magazines.

Oddsocks

Do you have a bedroom of your very own? I hope it's not untidy like this one.
How many pairs of socks can you see? Is there one odd sock left over?
Here's something you could do with it.

Slip your hand inside.
Hello sock!

Paste on some coloured sticky
spots to make eyes and a nose.

Dab a little paste on top
of his head and stick on
wool for hair.

Would your sock like to have
cloth ears or even a cotton-wool
beard?

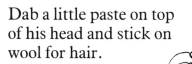

Have fun with your Oddsocks friends.

Mixing Magic

Next time you're painting pictures, try mixing a little magic like the
Paintbox Wizard.

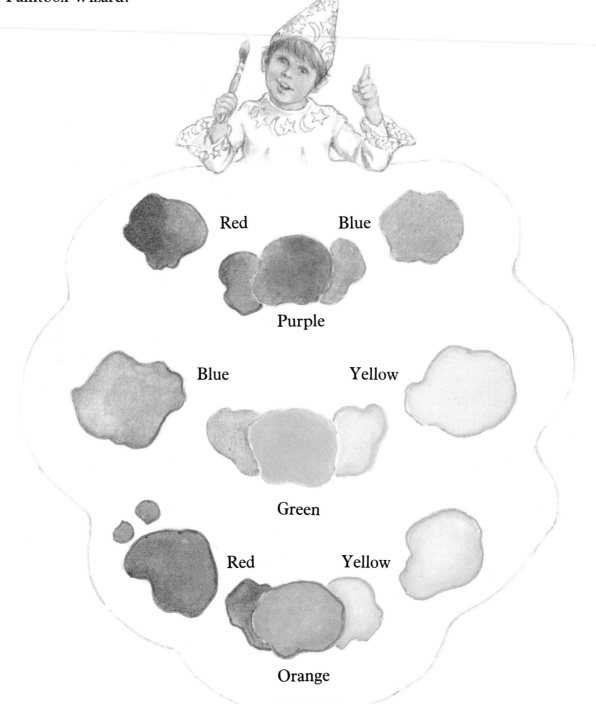

Red   Blue

Purple

Blue   Yellow

Green

Red   Yellow

Orange

Did you know that when you mix two colours together you can make a new one
that's quite different. Go on – you try it!

But don't forget to wear an apron or you might end up looking like the Paintbox
Wizard. I wonder what his mum is going to say?

Rainbow Pots

Mix up pots of all the new colours you can make. Pin up your biggest sheet of paper and paint an . . .

Red and yellow and pink and green,
Orange and purple and blue,
I can sing a rainbow,
Sing a rainbow.
Sing a rainbow too.

Listen with your eyes, O listen with your eyes
And sing everything you see.
Sing a rainbow,
Sing a rainbow,
Sing along with me.

Red and yellow and pink and green,
Orange and purple and blue,
I can sing a rainbow,
Sing a rainbow.
Sing a rainbow too.

Andrew's New Plate

Ever since he was very small, Andrew had had his own special plate. It was a beautiful plate, bright yellow with rabbits running round the edge.

Andrew used his rabbit plate for every meal. He ate his breakfast toast off it. He ate his lunchtime fish fingers off it. He ate his scrambled eggs off it at tea-time.

He even took the plate with him when they went to visit Gran.

Then one day something dreadful happened. Andrew and his mum and dad and big sister Ellen went to Gran's for lunch. After lunch they were all going to a Jumble Sale in the Church Hall. Andrew took two things with him. One was his ten pence pocket money and the other was his plate for lunch. Mum wrapped the big round plate in a teacloth and popped it into her bag. Andrew put the little round ten pence in his pocket.

When he got to Gran's he took out the ten pence to show her. It was bright and round and shining silver. Mum took out the plate. It was still wrapped in the cloth, but it was not round any more. It was broken into five jagged pieces, just like a jigsaw puzzle.

Andrew WAS upset.

"Never mind," said Mum. "We can always stick the bits together again but it will come unstuck if we try to wash it. We'll have to find you another plate."

"Don't want one!" said Andrew. He would eat no lunch, not even when Gran put it on one of her best plates with the roses round the rim. He wanted his own yellow rabbit plate or nothing at all.

At the Jumble Sale, after lunch, it was very busy. People kept bumping into Andrew and someone knocked him on the head with an old lamp-shade.

"Come and help me to find a bike," said Mum. Andrew shook his head.

"I'm looking for a lawnmower," said Dad. "Like to come and help me?" But Andrew shook his head again.

"I'm going to the bric-a-brac stall," said Ellen, vanishing into the crowd.

"What's bric-a-brac?" Andrew asked.

"Bits and things," said Mum.

"Odds and bobs," said Dad. Just then Ellen came hurrying back.

"Come and see this, Andrew," she panted. "There's something you might like." She pulled him into the crowd round the table and shoved him to the front. There were some very odd things on the bric-a-brac stall.

A big black and white china dog with one ear missing stared down at him. It looked as if it was listening to something. Behind it were boxes and brushes and jugs and bottles and little bowls and cups of all shapes and sizes and colours. Right at the back, on top of a wobbly pile of dishes, there was a plate.

It was a big round blue and white plate with a picture that looked very interesting. There were trees and a river with a bridge and boats. On the other side of the bridge was a street full of funny little houses with tiny windows. Coming down the street, in the middle of the picture, was a coach pulled by four horses. Everything on the plate – houses, the little bridge, even the trees – was all blue and white.

"It's got blue horses!" said Andrew.

"And people," said Ellen. The man sitting on the coach had a fat blue face. "It's only ten pence. You could buy it."

Andrew gave the lady his little round silver ten pence and she put the big round plate in a paper bag.

"Would you like your big sister to carry it?" she asked.

"*I'll* carry it," said Andrew. And he did. He carried it very carefully all the way back to Gran's house.

Gran filled a basin with soapy water and tied an apron round him. Andrew knelt on a chair to give his new plate a really good scrub. He polished the trees, the little bridge and the river until they shone. He gave a special polish to the man with the fat blue face and the houses with the tiny windows. Then he looked at the picture.

"Who lives in the houses?" he asked.

"Don't know," said Mum. "Who do you think?" Andrew looked at his plate for a long time.

"Rabbits," he whispered. Then he sat down and ate a very big meal of sausages and beans and mashed potatoes off his new blue plate.

45

A Great Big Super

Is there a fairground near you? Ask your friends to help you make these funny clowns. Use shiny sweet papers for balloons, and paint their faces on white paper plates.

Five jolly clowns,
Clattered through the door.
One fell off the Crazy Car,
And that left four.

Four jolly clowns,
Playing 'Can't Catch Me.'
One slipped on a banana skin,
And that left three.

Three jolly clowns,
One with big blue shoes.
Someone tied his laces together,
And that left two.

Two jolly clowns,
With some custard pies to fling.
One ducked – the other didn't,
And that left one.

One jolly clown,
Standing on his hands.
Up jumped the other four
And – CLATTER – down he lands!

Summer Picture

Use wool and cloth from your Patch Box to make hair and clothes. You could cut out flowers from wrapping paper or old magazines to decorate their hats.
Don't forget to paint a big tent with flags.

Here's another action rhyme.

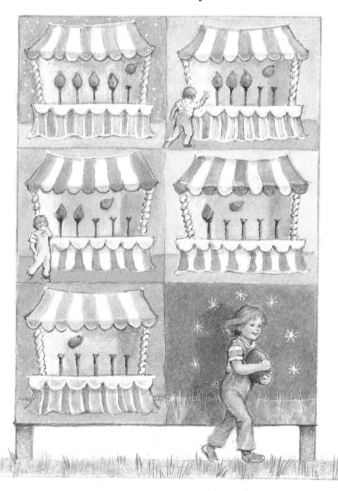

Five brown coconuts
Sitting in a row,
Throw a ball – knock one down.
Now there's only four.

Four brown coconuts,
That's all I can see,
Throw a ball – knock one down.
Now there's only three.

Three brown coconuts,
This is what you do,
Throw a ball – knock one down.
Now there's only two.

Two brown coconuts,
Sitting in the sun,
Throw a ball – knock one down.
Now there's only one.

One brown coconut,
Goodness what a size!
Throw a ball – knock it down.
Hooray, you've won a prize!

Secret Garden

Do you have some little dolls who would like a garden of their own?

You can make one from an old dish or basin. Cover the bottom with small stones to help drain the water away. Plants don't like wet feet. Now fill it to the top with earth and your garden is ready to plant.

Perhaps someone who has a rockery might give you some very small flowers. Plant them carefully and don't forget to water them. Thick moss makes a soft green lawn with a large flat shell or tin foil dish as a pool.
Give the dolls tables and chairs made from cotton reels or bricks and they will enjoy sitting in the sunshine.

48   Goodness, that's a funny flower to find in a small garden.

Shadow Play

Is it sunny enough for your shadow to come out to play? Can you hide from it? Where has it gone? I wonder what makes a shadow. Do you know?

My Shadow

I have a little shadow that goes in and out
with me
And what can be the use of him is more than I
can see.
He is very, very like me from the heels up to
the head;
And I see him jump before me, when I jump
into my bed.

The funniest thing about him is the way he
likes to grow –
Not at all like proper children, which is always
very slow;
For he sometimes shoots up taller like an india-
rubber ball,
And he sometimes gets so little that there's
none of him at all.

One morning, very early, before the sun was
up,
I rose and found the shining dew on every
buttercup;
But my lazy little shadow, like an arrant
sleepyhead,
Had stayed at home behind me and was fast
asleep in bed.

ROBERT LOUIS STEVENSON

49

Play Boxes

Do you have some toys looking for a new house? Let's help them to find one.

Choose a big square empty box and paint the inside a bright colour.

Cut out pictures of doors and windows from an old magazine and paste them into your room.

Use squares of coloured cloth or paper from your Patch Box as carpets and make furniture from little boxes or building bricks. Wouldn't you like to live in there too?

If you use lots of boxes you can build all sorts of things.

A block of flats . . . or a row of shops. I wonder who went for the shopping by helicopter?

Use building bricks as petrol pumps in your garage, and make a car wash with empty toilet roll holders covered with stuck-on wool from your Patch Box.
There's plenty of space on the roof for a big car park.
Whoops! There's that helicopter again!

Do you think you could make a Police Station, a Fire Station or a Hospital?

Beech Leaves

In autumn down the beechwood path
The leaves lie thick upon the ground.
It's there I love to kick my way
And hear their crisp and crashing sound.

I am a giant, and my steps
Echo and thunder to the sky.
How the small creatures of the woods
Must quake and cower as I pass by!

This brave and merry noise I make
In summer also when I stride
Down to the shining, pebbly sea
And kick the frothing waves aside.

JAMES REEVES

Blow, wind, blow and go, mill, go
That the miller may grind his corn,
That the baker may take it,
And into bread make it,
And bring us a loaf in the morn.

TRAD.

AUTUMN

The boughs do shake and the bells do
ring,
So merrily comes our harvest in,
Our harvest in, our harvest in,
So merrily comes our harvest in.

We have ploughed, we have sowed,
We have reaped, we have mowed,
We have brought home every load,
Hip, hip, hip, harvest home!

TRAD.

Autumn

Yellow the bracken,
Golden the sheaves,
Rosy the apples,
Crimson the leaves;
Mist on the hillside,
Clouds grey and white.
Autumn good morning!
Summer good night.

FLORENCE HOATSON

Let's go down to the park today.
How many children have come to play?
How many ducks on the pond can you see?
Count them slowly, one, two, three.

Look at the park when it starts to rain!
Come on, Mum, hurry home again.
What do you think — is it too wet to stay?
You can always come back another day.

Snowdrop Surprises

Help Mum to buy some snowdrop bulbs. Then find a deep bowl and make a cosy bed of bulb fibre in the bottom.

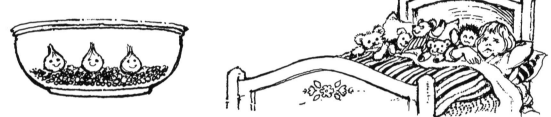

Tuck your bulbs into the fibre. Remember to leave plenty of room between them. You wouldn't like to be squashed out of bed would you?

Cover the bulbs with a fibre quilt, give them a little water to drink and pop them into a dark place to sleep. Shhhhhh!

One day – if you remember to keep them watered – your bulbs will begin to wake up and grow.

Bread . . .

In the autumn when the farmer's field of corn has grown tall and golden he cuts it down.

The harvesting machine separates the ears of corn from the stalks. The ears of corn are put in bags and taken to . . .

. . . the miller, who grinds up the corn in his mill to make a fine white powder called flour. The flour is put in bags and taken to . . .

. . . the baker, who mixes it with yeast and water to make – bread.

Pat a cake, pat a cake, baker's van,
Bring me a loaf as fast as you can.
Slice it and wrap it and sell it to me,
So I can have baked beans on toast for my tea.   MOIRA MILLER

Here's another busy farmer – he has some cows.
Every morning and evening he milks the cows and sends the milk to the dairy.

Some of the milk is put into bottles. Some cream from the cow's milk is made into butter in the factory.
You could make your own butter at home.

Pour a little pot of double cream into an empty jar.

Make sure the lid fits very tightly.

Then shake,

and shake

and shake

and shake the little jar.

. . . And Butter

At first nothing seems to happen . . .

but suddenly

the cream turns into solid lumps with some thin runny buttermilk.

Pour off the milk – you can drink it. Do you like the taste?

Tip the little lump of butter onto a plate. Sometimes the dairy adds salt. You could sprinkle on just a little.

Pat your butter into a square shape with a knife.

Let it sit in a cold place for a few minutes.

Then spread it on some bread and eat it. YUM!

The North Wind and the Sun

Have you ever been out on one of those days when the weather doesn't seem to be able to make its mind up what it's going to do next? One minute it's sunny, the next it's raining, then you've no sooner got your wellingtons on, when the sun comes out and dries up all the puddles.

This is a story about a day just like that.

The North Wind woke up early in his cave up among the high mountains and came storming down the valley looking for fun.

Whooooooooooosh!

"Drat that wind," said a lady chasing her best hat along the road.

"Oh help!" said a tall gentleman as his umbrella turned inside-out for the third time that morning.

"No fish today, boys!" said the skipper of a little fishing boat out at sea and he turned back to harbour, bouncing through the grey stormy waves.

But the North Wind didn't care!

"I Am The Greatest!" he howled. "There's nobody in the whole world stronger than me!" Just to prove it he blew the weathercock off the top of the church steeple.

"He needs taking down a peg or two," said the South Wind, curled up quietly on a little cloud.

"You're right of course," said the Sun. "I've a good mind to do it myself. He's such a show-off."

"Wha-a-a-a-t's that you said?" roared the North Wind, whistling up, scattering clouds and rain and hail in all directions at once.

"Puff, puff. I said you're just a show-off," said the Sun. "All this boasting about being the Greatest! All puff and piffle."

The North Wind roared himself into a great hurricane of fury.

"I AM THE GREATEST!!" he stormed, and the chimney pots for miles around went flying.

"Well then," said the Sun. "Prove it."

"Prrrrroooove it?" roared the North Wind.

"Yes," said the Sun. "Look. Do you see that man down there? The one in the big heavy black coat?"

"I can see him," howled the North Wind. "What about it?"

"If you really are the Greatest let's see you blow that coat off him," said the Sun.

"Easy-peasy!" said the North Wind. "Is that all? Stand back and watch the fun."

The Sun slipped quietly behind a cloud and watched. The North Wind whirled round a few times, and then he blew. He raged down the street, tumbling flowerpots, tossing bushes, blowing the leaves off the trees, and caught and tugged the man with the heavy black coat.

"What a storm," said the man. He turned up his collar and pulled the coat tighter round him. Up on her cloud the Sun gave a little chuckle.

"Humph," sniffed the North Wind. "Just wait. I'll have that coat off him in no time." He roared up to the other end of the street, to get a good run at it, and went storming back down again, whistling and screaming.

"I've never known a storm like it," said the man. He buttoned the coat right up to his neck and pulled the belt even tighter. The North Wind stormed and ranted and raved and blew fit to bust. He knocked over fences and even blew down an old garden hut. But the man only tucked his hands deep down into the pockets, and shivered.

The North Wind, completely out of puff, flopped down in a field of flattened grass.

"Right," said the Sun quietly. "Now it's my turn."

She slid gently out from behind her cloud and spread her heat around the man. He stopped, and looked up in amazement at the clear blue sky and the Sun's bright golden smile.

"Oh my," he said. "But it's a very odd day. One minute blowing a gale, the next like midsummer." He walked on down the road.

The sun laughed and grew hotter and hotter. The man unbuttoned his heavy black coat.

"It is warm," he said, and turned down the thick collar.

The Sun chuckled quietly, and the birds joined in.

"What a wonderful day it's turned into," said the man. "It's far too hot for this old coat." And he stopped — and took off his heavy black coat.

"Now who's the Greatest?" beamed the Sun, and the bright blue sky was filled with her smile.

"Humph!" muttered the North Wind, and he puffed back up to his rocky cave in the mountains, but he still comes storming back down sometimes. I wonder if he'll come out today. What do you think?

Windy Weather

Where does the wind come from? Can you see it?

Or taste it?

Or smell it?

So how do you know it's there at all?

Wind on the Hill

No one can tell me,
Nobody knows,
Where the wind comes from,
Where the wind goes.

It's flying somewhere
As fast as it can,
I couldn't keep up with it,
Not if I ran.

But if I stopped holding
The string of my kite,
It would blow with the wind
For a day and a night.

A.A. MILNE

Balloons, Birds and Bugs

Blow up a balloon . . . bigger . . . and bigger . . . AND BIGGER!!

But DON'T LET GO!!

Ask someone to help you to tie it up very tightly.

Now you have a bouncing balloon. But what did you fill it up with?

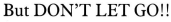

Cut out some paper wings and tape them to your balloon to make a bird or a funny bug. You can draw eyes and a mouth with a felt pen. Who do you think has the most Ugly Bug here?

Monster Masks

Would you like to turn into a monster? How would you do it?

Find a magician to help you?

No!

Find a brown PAPER bag, crayons, sellotape, scissors and coloured paper?

Yes!

Pop the bag over your head. Ask Mum to make pencil marks where your eyes are then take it off and cut out two round holes. Now you can decorate your mask. Stick on silver paper to make a fish or a space monster. Cut fringes round the bottom and curl them around a pencil for hair or a beard. Are you going to make a friendly monster or a fierce monster?

What will Mum say?

Hello, Monster. Would you like some orange juice?

64   PLEASE REMEMBER: Never use a plastic bag to make a mask.

Hallowe'en

It would be fun to have a Fancy Dress Party for Hallowe'en. Ask your friends to dress up as witches and ghosts and come for a Spooky Tea.

The Ghost

Look out
Look out
There's a ghost about,
Howling, horrible hulabaloos.
It's wearing a bed-cover over its head
And what looks like my grandmother's shoes.

Look out
Look out
We haven't a doubt
That it's silly old Millicent Mary.
But we still huddle up in a giggling gaggle
'Cos it's fun in a way, feeling scary.

Witch, Witch

"Witch, witch, where do you fly?"
'Under the clouds and over the sky.'

"Witch, witch, what do you eat?"
'Little black apples from Hurricane Street.'

"Witch, witch, what do you drink?"
'Vinegar, blacking and good red ink.'

"Witch, witch, where do you sleep?"
'Up in the clouds where pillows are cheap.'

ROSE FYLEMAN   65

Spooky Party

Here are some games to play at your Hallowe'en Spooky Party.

Dooking for Apples:
Fill a basin with water and put it on a plastic cloth on the floor. Float some apples in the water. Can you drop in a fork and catch one?

Guess What's Gone: Ask Mum to put some small things on a tray. Look at it very carefully for half a minute. Let Mum cover it with a cloth and take one thing away. Guess what's gone!

Make a Spooky Face Tea with mashed potato and little sausages. What would he taste like with Baked Bean hair?

Ghastly Ghosts: Who-o-o-os the best painter? Give everyone a big sheet of black paper and some white paint. Who do you think has painted the spookiest ghost?

Musical Bumps in the Night: When the music stops playing everyone sits on a cushion. But there are five children and only four cushions! Who's going to be left out? When the music starts again make it four children and three cushions. Go on playing the game until there's only one child left.

Don't forget to wave goodbye to your witches, ghosts and guests and say thank you for coming.

Dough Doodles

Here's some magic you can do with just flour and water. It can be a bit messy so don't forget to ask Mum to help you.

Take a big bowl and put in eight spoonfuls of flour. Can you count them yourself?

Try to roll the flour up into a ball. It won't go will it? What a fluffy flop!

Now pour in some water.

Not too little!

Not too much!

Use just enough and you can squeeze the flour into a ball of dough. What can you make with it? If you want to make your dough last for a few days mix some salt into the flour and keep it in a plastic bag in the fridge.

68

Silly Spoons

Are there any old wooden spoons in the kitchen? Ask Mum if she'll let you have one then you can make a Silly Spoon Puppet.

Draw a face on the back of the spoon with felt pens.

Stick on some wool from your Patch Box using sellotape, to make hair.

Wrap a clean duster or an old scrap of cloth round the spoon.

You can fasten it on with tape or an elastic band.
    Hello Silly Spoons!

Can you make a spoon that's sad on one side and happy on the other? Or make a Sleepy Spoon that's wide awake on one side and sleeping on the other.

A Great Big Super

Collect as many different coloured autumn leaves as you can find. Make sure they are all dry and sort them in your Patch Box. Can you find nuts and dried grass as well?

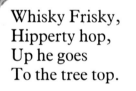

Whisky Frisky,
Hipperty hop,
Up he goes
To the tree top.

Whirly twirly,
Round and round,
Down he scampers,
To the ground.

Furly curly,
What a tail;
Tall as a feather,
Broad as a sail.

Where's his supper?
In the shell.
Snappy cracky,
Out it fell.

I had a little nut tree,
Nothing would it bear,
But a silver nutmeg
And a golden pear.
The King of Spain's daughter
Came to visit me,
And all for the sake of
My little nut tree.

I skipped over water,
I danced over sea,
And all the birds in the air
Couldn't catch me.

TRAD.

TRAD.

70

Autumn Picture

Paint or crayon trees with long branches on a big sheet of brown paper then stick the dried leaves back on again to make an autumn picture. Can you make a squirrel out of fluffy brown wool?

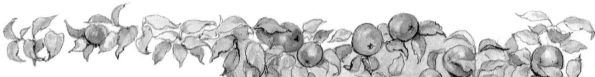

Down in the Orchard

Down in the orchard
It's harvest time
And up the tall ladders
The fruit pickers climb.

Among the green branches
That sway overhead
The apples are hanging
All rosy and red,

Just ripe for the picking
All juicy and sweet,
So pretty to look at
And lovely to eat.

ANON.

Five little owls in an old elm-tree,
Fluffy and puffy as owls could be,
Blinking and winking with big round eyes
At the big round moon that hung in the skies;
As I passed beneath, I could hear one say,
"There'll be mouse for supper, there will, today."
Then all of them hooted, "Tu whit, tu whoo!
Yes, mouse for supper, Hoo hoo, Hoo hoo!"

ANON.

Winter Morning

Winter is the king of showmen
Turning tree stumps into snowmen
And houses into birthday cakes
And spreading sugar over lakes.
Smooth and clean and frosty white,
The world looks good enough to bite.
That's the season to be young,
Catching snow flakes on your tongue.

Snow is snowy when it's snowing,
I'm sorry it's slushy when it's going.

OGDEN NASH

The north wind doth blow,
And we shall have snow,
And what will poor Robin do then,
    poor thing?
He'll sit in a barn,
And keep himself warm
And tuck his head under his wing,
    poor thing.

WINTER

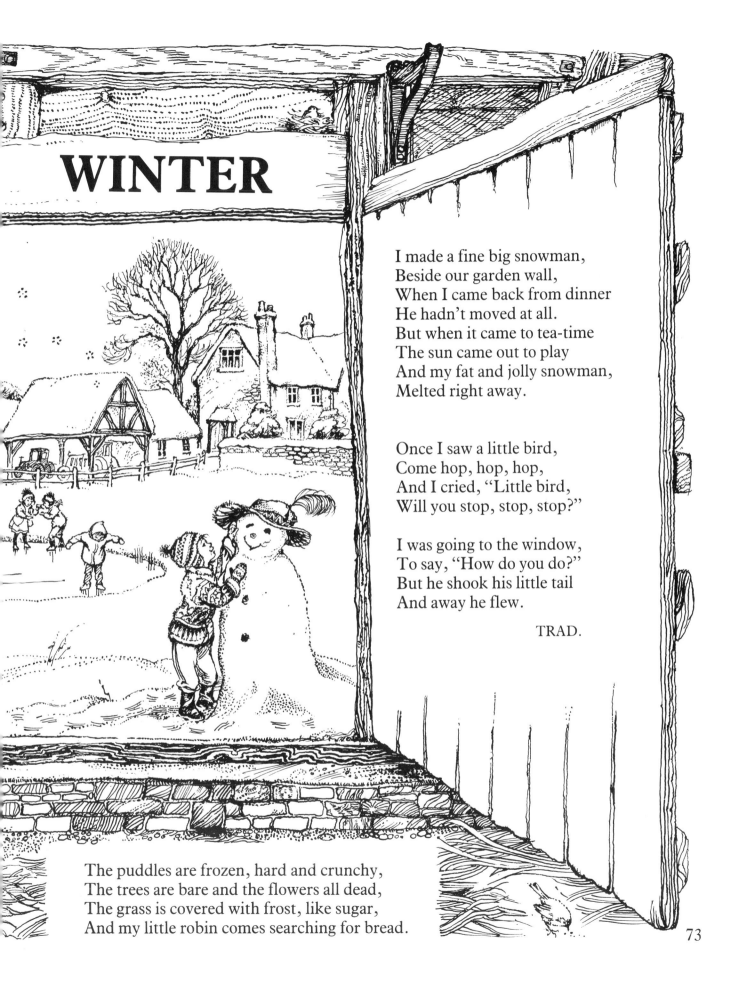

I made a fine big snowman,
Beside our garden wall,
When I came back from dinner
He hadn't moved at all.
But when it came to tea-time
The sun came out to play
And my fat and jolly snowman,
Melted right away.

Once I saw a little bird,
Come hop, hop, hop,
And I cried, "Little bird,
Will you stop, stop, stop?"

I was going to the window,
To say, "How do you do?"
But he shook his little tail
And away he flew.

TRAD.

The puddles are frozen, hard and crunchy,
The trees are bare and the flowers all dead,
The grass is covered with frost, like sugar,
And my little robin comes searching for bread.

Let's go down to the park today.
How many children have come to play?
How many ducks on the pond can you see?
Count them slowly, one, two, three.

Look at the park when it starts to rain.
Come on, Mum, hurry home again!
What do you think, is it too wet to stay?
You can always come back another day.

Baked Potato

Take a big potato, scrub it very clean and dry it with a cloth. Poke a row of little holes along the top with a fork. Be careful now!

Wrap the potato in a sheet of tinfoil – it looks like a space spud now – and ask Mum to pop it into a medium hot oven, on the middle shelf.

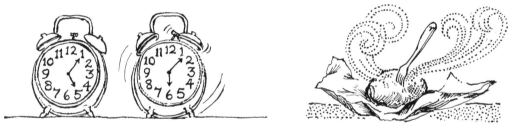

Wait for an hour – sometimes really big potatoes take longer – then ask Mum to take the potato out of the oven and unwrap it. You can test if it's ready by sticking in a fork. If it's soft you can eat it. Watch out though, it's hot.

Mmmm! That smells delicious. Cut your potato open and put in some salt and a little bit of butter or a spoonful of grated cheese, or some warm baked beans.

Hot Drinks

Put a cupful of milk into a little pan and ask Dad to help you heat it.
Pour it very carefully back into your mug and stir in two teaspoonfuls
of Drinking Chocolate. That smells good!

Crumble an Oxo cube into a mug and ask Dad to pour in some hot water.
Stir it until the cube has all dissolved. Add a little sprinkle of salt and drink
up. Aaaah – very tasty!

For a really good bedtime drink warm up a mugful of milk, and stir in a
teaspoonful of clear honey.
    I bet the bears would like some too!

Ship Shapes

I saw three ships come sailing by,
On Christmas Day, on Christmas Day,
I saw three ships come sailing by,
On Christmas Day in the morning.

TRAD.

Can you match these shapes to the ships?

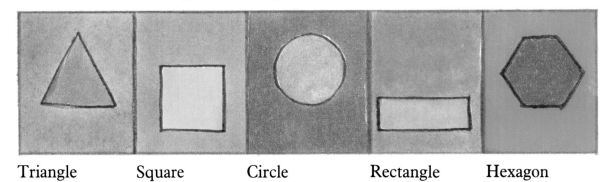

Triangle   Square   Circle   Rectangle   Hexagon

Igloos

If your little ships could sail away to the Far and Frozen North they would come to the land of the Eskimos who live in houses made of ice. If you know any small eskimos you could build an ice house for them.

You need lots and lots of ice cubes from the fridge or freezer. Tip them out on to a plastic tray.

Build a ring of cubes around your little Eskimo. You can make the cubes stick together if you sprinkle them with salt.

Keep building it higher and making your igloo smaller towards the top.

If you put food colouring in the water before you freeze the cubes you can have a coloured house.

I wonder what would happen if you leave it sitting in the kitchen all night?

Ben's Bird Bells

"Bother those birds," said Mum, lifting the milk bottles from the front door step. "They've done it again!"

Every single milk bottle had a little round hole in the silver top. The birds had made the holes so that they could steal the milk.

"Why do they do that?" asked Ben.

"They're hungry," said Dad.

"We'll put out some scraps for them," said Mum.

After breakfast she and Ben collected together all the pieces of toast that were left – even the crusts that Ben didn't want to eat. Dad added a little bit of bacon and a handful of cornflakes, put everything on a big plate and Ben took it out to the garden.

"Scatter it on the ground under the tree," said Mum. "The birds will see it there."

Ben put the scraps on the hard spiky frozen grass under the tree, then he went back into the house to watch what would happen.

Someone else though was watching what happened. And that someone else was next door's big white cat! She watched, and she waited. But the birds could see her, so none of them came down for the food.

"Bother," said Ben. "The birds don't want the food."

"Bother," thought the big white cat, and because she couldn't catch a bird she ate up the scraps instead.

"Bother," said Mum the next morning, because the milk bottle tops all had holes in them again.

"Perhaps we could hang up a net of nuts for the birds," said Dad. "Then the cat wouldn't be able to scare them away."

"Good idea," said Mum.

In the supermarket she and Ben bought a little red net stuffed full of peanuts.

"I like peanuts," said Ben, as they hung it up on the tree.

"So do the birds!" said Mum, so Ben went back into the house to watch what would happen.

But someone else was watching what happened. And that someone was the little grey squirrel who lived in the trees down the road. He watched and he waited, and when there was no-one in the garden, and the road was very quiet, he climbed down the tree to the branch where the nuts were.

He pulled and chewed and nibbled at the net. The birds sat in the top of the tree chirping and whistling to each other.

"Look at that squirrel," they whistled. "Look what he's doing."

But the squirrel didn't care about them. He nibbled and gnawed at that net until at last it fell to the ground. Quick as a flash down the tree he ran. He grabbed the bag of nuts and scampered off with them.

"Bother," said Ben. "He's stolen all the nuts."

"Bother that squirrel," chirped the birds. "He's gone off with our breakfast."

"Bother," said Mum the next morning, because the milk bottles had no tops left on them at all. The birds had taken them right off.

"I don't know what to do," said Mum.

"It's easy," said the little old lady next door. "Make bird bells."

"Bird bells?" said Mum and Ben together. "What are bird bells?"

"Come and see," said the little old lady, and she took them into her back garden. In the middle of the grass, on the tree where the apples grew in summer time, there were lots of little bells. There were white bells and blue bells, silver bells and bells that were all colours. They swung from the branches on pieces of coloured wool and hanging from some of them were little birds.

The birds held on with their claws, swinging backwards and forwards and pecking at something inside the bells.

"What are they doing?" asked Ben.

"Having breakfast," said the old lady. "Come and see." In the kitchen she opened the door of her fridge and took out a tray. On the tray there were four plastic yoghurt pots and two little silver tart cups, filled with something hard and white and lumpy.

"That's fat," said the little old lady. "All melted together and mixed up with nuts and bread and oats and scraps of this and that. Just what birds like best."

"And poured into the pots to set hard," said Mum.

"Yes," said the little old lady. "But first you must pop a loop of wool through the bottom so that you can hang it up."

She turned one of the little pots upside down and there was a loop of red wool.

"You can have that one," she said to Ben.

"And can we make some more at home?" said Ben.

"Of course," said Mum.

They hung up the little bird bell in the garden and Ben went back into the house to watch what would happen.

"Bother," said the big white cat looking up at the bird bell. "I can't get up there." She went back off to her own garden.

"Bother," said the squirrel. "It's right out on the end of a twig, and I'll fall off if I try to get to it."

"Beeeeeautiful," chirruped the birds, and they fluttered into Ben's garden to swing on the bell and eat the nuts and fat.

"Oh – bother," said Ben's mum next morning, because the birds had pecked holes in all the milk bottles again!

But she didn't really mind.

Bird Bells

It's very easy to make some bird bells like Ben's. Ask Mum to help you.

Collect some tinfoil cake cups. Poke a little hole in the bottom of each one, ask Mum to push some thread through and tie it round a used match.

Put a 2oz piece of fat in a heatproof bowl. Stand the bowl in a pan of hot water and wait until the fat melts.

Chop some nuts, bread, cheese and scraps of bacon and dried fruits into small pieces. Remember to be careful with the knife.

Stir all the chopped food into the bowl of melted fat. Make sure it is well mixed in then fill the tinfoil cups and leave them in a cold place.

Once the fat has set hard you can hang up the bird bells. Decorate a special Christmas tree for the birds and they will sing you a thank you song. Don't forget to give them a dish of water as well.

Feed the Birds

In the winter time birds need food and water. Put the water in a wide shallow dish:
an old baking tin is a good idea. If it freezes into ice remember to tip it out
and put in fresh water.

Large birds can eat scraps
of food from the tray.

Little birds can hang
on the bird bells and
nut bag.

Come here, little robin, and don't
    be afraid,
I would not hurt even a feather;
Come here, little Robin, and pick
    up some food,
To feed you this very cold weather.

The winter has come, but it will not
    stay long,
And the summer we soon shall be greeting;
Then remember, dear Robin, to sing me
    a song,
In return for the breakfast you're eating.

Two little dickie birds
Sitting on a wall,
One named Peter, one named Paul.
Fly away Peter, fly away Paul.
Come back Peter, come back Paul.

ANON.

83

Puppet Pantomime

Have you ever been to a Christmas Pantomime? Here's one you can make for yourself.

Find a big empty square box. Ask Mum to help you cut a square hole in the front. Now you have a stage.

But how will your puppets get on to the stage? You will have to cut a narrow slot down each side of the box.

You can find pantomime people in old magazines. Cut them out and paste them on to thin card so that they will stand up.

Sellotape long strips of stiff cardboard on to your puppets. Now you can slide them on to your stage, to act in the pantomime.

Old calendar pictures make very good scenery and your theatre would look even better if you painted the box and stuck on coloured shapes.

Are you going to make tickets so that everyone can come and see your pantomime?

Musical Pots and Tops

Ask Mum for some empty milk bottles. Pour a little water into the first one, more into the second and even more into the third.
Tap gently on the bottles with a teaspoon. They make different sounds.
Can you make up a tune with your bottles?

Tape together two empty yoghurt pots with a few dried beans inside.
What sort of sound does that make when you shake it? Try making different sounding shakers with small stones or buttons.
Can you make a noise like giant footsteps or a horse galloping?

Thread clean milk bottle tops on to some wool and tie the ends together to make a jingler. Does it sound like raindrops? Use all your pots and tops to make the sounds for your pantomime puppets.

Warm and Woolly

Happiness

John had
Great big
Waterproof
Boots on;
John had a
Great big
Waterproof
Hat;
John had a
Great big
Waterproof
Mackintosh –
And that
(Said John)
   Is
   That.

A.A. MILNE

The Mitten Song

"Thumbs in the thumb place,
Fingers all together!"
This is the song
We sing in mitten-weather
When it is cold,
It doesn't matter whether
Mittens are wool,
Or made of finest leather.
This is the song,
We sing in mitten-weather.
"Thumbs in the thumb place,
Fingers all together!"

MARIE LOUISE ALLEN

Furry Bear

If I were a bear
And a big bear too,
I shouldn't much care
If it froze or snew;
I shouldn't much mind
If it snowed or friz –
I'd be all fur lined
With a coat like his!
For I'd have fur boots and a brown fur wrap,
And brown fur knickers and a big fur cap.
I'd have a fur muffle-ruff to cover my jaws,
And brown fur mittens on my big brown paws.
With a big brown furry-down up to my head,
I'd sleep all the winter in a big fur bed.

A.A. MILNE

Dressing Up

John's going down to the park to play
On a cold and frosty winter day.

Should he wear a T shirt, a woolly or vest?
Which do you think would be the best?

Long or short? Which pants to put on?
It's cold outside. Better wrap up, John!

Wellingtons, sandals or new blue shoes?
I wonder if you can help him choose.

Hat, jacket and mitts and off you go.
All ready at last to play in the snow.

Why the Pine Tree is Always Green

Once upon a cold day, as the icy winds roared down from the high mountains, a little bird flew from tree to tree. He was looking for a home for the winter. He came to a beech tree growing in the forest.

"Beautiful Beech Tree," said the little bird, "may I come and live among your golden leaves until the Spring?"

"No – certainly not!" answered the Beech Tree. "I have the most beautiful leaves in the forest. I cannot give a home to a scruffy little bird like you."

Sadly the little bird flew to a tall oak that stood alone in a field.

"Mighty Oak Tree," whispered the little bird. "May I shelter among your strong branches until the winter is over?"

"I am the King of Trees," said the Oak Tree. "It would not do to have a scruffy little bird like you among my fine branches."

The little bird flew on, searching for a home. But everywhere he went the answer was the same. Even the gentle willow tree by the river was so busy admiring her reflection in the water that she did not hear the little bird.

Through fields and gardens, woods and farms he flew, and at last came to rest on the dark, sweet-smelling green branches of a pine tree.

"Tall Pine Tree," said the little bird. "May I live among your thick green needles? The cold winter is coming and I must find somewhere safe and warm to make my home."

"Of course," nodded the tall Pine Tree. Then his friend the Spruce Tree who grew in the same forest leaned across.

"I too will protect you, little bird," he said. "For like my brother the Pine I am tall and strong."

Not to be outdone the tiny Juniper bush at their feet waved his shining berries.

"I will give you food for the winter, little bird," he called.

The little bird lived happily through the long cold autumn days. Winter came, and with it the Wild North Wind and Jack Frost. Together they tossed the ships at sea, tugged the branches of the trees, and froze the fingers and toes of the children until they had to run and jump to keep warm.

"Look," said the Wild North Wind, sweeping through the forest one day. "Look how the Pine and the Spruce and the tiny Juniper have given shelter to the little bird when the other trees would not. How cruel they were. Let us blow away their leaves so that they will feel the winter

cold!" So Jack Frost nipped and the Wild North Wind blew until all the golden beech leaves, the yellow oak leaves, and even the silver leaves of the willow tree blew off down the river.

But they left the thick green needles on the Pine Tree and the Spruce and the tiny Juniper to protect the little bird. That is why, to this day, Christmas pine trees always have thick green needles in winter when the other trees have no leaves at all.

Footprints

Feet in the snow and mud.
Who's been here?

Which way did they go?
Are they far or near?

Follow the footprints, it's easy to do,
But look behind – who's
following you?

90

Paint Prints

Ask Mum to let you have a polystyrene supermarket tray, and wash it clean.

Fold a piece of kitchen paper and lay it on the tray. Mix up some paint and pour it into the tray.

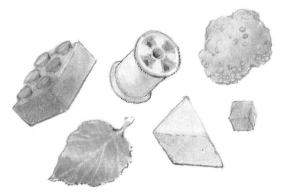

You can use all sorts of things to print patterns. Try corks, leaves, cotton reels, bricks, sponge.

Dip the shapes in the paint and then press them gently onto a sheet of thick paper. Make sure you cover the table with newspapers first.

You could use your paint prints to make Christmas cards, decorations or wrapping paper for presents.

Don't forget to wear an apron, you don't want a paint printed pullover too!

A Great Big Super Winter Picture

Pin up a great big sheet of paper and paint or crayon a Christmas tree.
Decorate your tree with milk bottle tops, pieces of Christmas ribbon, cut out pictures from wrapping paper and photographs of toys from old magazines.

A Garland of Evergreen

Let's make a garland for
Christmas
Of evergreen tied in a ring,
With berries and baubles and candles;
Let's twine it with tinselly string.

Let's make a garland for
Christmas
And hang it for people to see,
To wish them the happiest Christmas,
From you, and the garland and me.

Make some holly ring decorations with empty cheese boxes or paper plates. Paste on green tissue circles for leaves and use red stick-on spots for berries.

92   HILDA I. ROSTRON

and Some Christmas Decorations

Ask Mum to help you cut out and fold a Cracker Christmas Card then colour it with your crayons or paints.

Christmas Pudding

Into the pudding put the plums,
Stir about, stir about, stir about all.

Next the good white flour comes,
Stir about, stir about, stir about all.

Sugar and peel and eggs and spice,
Stir about, stir about, stir about all.

This is the way our pudding's done,
Stir about, stir about, stir about all.

Try it yourself and have some fun,
Stir about, stir about, stir about all.

JENNY CHAPMAN

Make some paper birds like these. Decorate them with crayons and stuck on gold and silver stars and hang them up on a wire coat hanger.

Join strips of coloured sticky-backed paper together to make lots and lots of paper chains.

93

Me-Tree

Have you ever seen a photograph of your Mum when she was little?
Her Mum and Dad are your Gran and Grandad.
Your Dad's Mum and Dad are your Gran and Grandad too.

You can make your whole family into a tree.

Cut out 7 pieces of paper all the same size.
The backs of old Christmas cards are good.
Draw yourself on one card, Mum on the next,
then Dad and then both Grans and Grandads.

Use sellotape and string to fasten
the cards on to a wire coat-hanger.
Put yourself at the top with Mum
and Dad beneath. Hang Mum's Mum
and Dad on her card and Dad's on his.

Hang your Me-Tree where you can see it.

I wonder what would happen if your Grans and Grandads put up their
Mums and Dads too!

Bedtime

Star light, star bright,
First star I see tonight.
I wish I may, I wish I might,
Have the wish I wish tonight.

Twinkle twinkle little star
How I wonder what you are,
Up above the world so high,
Like a diamond in the sky.

In the dark blue sky you keep,
And often through my curtains peep,
For you never shut your eye,
Till the sun is in the sky.

JANE TAYLOR

After my bath
I try, try, try
To wipe myself
Till I'm dry, dry, dry.

Hands to wipe,
And fingers and toes,
And two wet legs
And shiny nose.

Just think how much
Less time I'd take
If I were a dog
And could shake, shake, shake.

AILEEN FISHER

Good night, sleep tight,
Happy dreams till morning bright.

MOIRA MILLER

A Note to Parents

I have tried to make this book as inexpensive to operate as possible. I know from my experience in playgroups that it is not necessary to spend a vast amount to make children happy. There are several things you will have to buy though and I have included them in a list below.

THINGS TO BUY

Poster Paints – It is best to buy these as tins of powder which can be mixed as and when required. Buy the basic red, blue, yellow, white and black and mix the other colours. (See page 42). Buy crayons and washable felt pens too.

Paint Brushes – Buy brushes with short chunky handles and good thick bristles. These are much easier for a small child to handle. Fun can be had too from old toothbrushes, pastry brushes, nail brushes etc.

Sellotape and Glue – Always buy washable, non-toxic School Glue. Sellotape is available in many colours and patterns, try some of these for a change.

Scissors – It is less frustrating for a child if you teach him how to use small sharp scissors, rather than the blunt plastic ones. As with any tool show him how to use them, supervise, but try not to interfere too much. Teach a child respect and he will handle tools responsibly.

THINGS NOT TO BUY

Empty washing-up bottles, yoghurt pots, polystyrene food trays, margarine and butter cartons.

Empty boxes of all sorts and sizes. Paper bags, cartons, toilet and kitchen roll inner tubes, egg packaging trays and boxes.

Polystyrene packaging chips, scraps of coloured cloth, wool, sweet wrappers, tin foil etc for the Patch Box (see page 16). In season the Patch Box can be filled with 'natural junk' – i.e. dried leaves, nuts, flower petals, pebbles, shells, small twigs, etc.

Paper – never underestimate how much you will need: Use wallpaper (try your local DIY shop for old pattern books), parcel wrapping, computer print-out, sugar paper. Lots and lots of old newspaper – cover every surface in sight before a child starts on a project and life will be easier all round!

And last but not least –
An old shirt or blouse worn back to front makes a very adequate coverall for a small child. If the sleeves are too long cut off the cuffs and thread elastic through them.

There are other materials used in the book from time to time, i.e. flour, salt, wooden spoons. I have not included these in the buying list as they are part of most kitchen supplies.

Good Luck and have fun together!

Moira Miller